CULTURE CHANGE

By Kimmy Nelson

Without Change There Is No Progress

"Culture Change" by Kimmy Nelson addresses current issues in our society that are or have caused problems for one or many people in their community or other populations throughout the earth.

In this book you will find religious conflicts of ideas, conflicts of interest relating to earth's energy resources, power, money climate and war, and you will also find answers for people who want to get out of the drug culture and strength for victims of Domestic Violence.

Dedicated to anyone who has ever recovered from drug or alcohol addiction, domestic violence or any other struggle that life dealt you.

Also in dedication to those who want to see change related to pollutions, wars, global leverage from Domestic Energy and global exports.

And Dedication to global evangelists, preachers and especially to missionaries who gave their lives for their religious beliefs.

Clashing Civilizations Or Culture Diversity

Samuel Huntington was certainly right about Civilization identity being more important in the future which is exactly what we see happening in Nevada with the ranchers verses Federal Bureau of Land Management sad to say! If the ranchers would have just complied to the law and paid their grazing fees none of the conflicts would have arisen.

Samuel Huntington was also right when he made a statement similar or to the effect of "People from different civilizations have different views on relations between God and man, persons and groups, ranchers or citizens and state, parents and children, husbands and wives, as well as differing views of civil rights and responsibilities, liberties and authority, equality and hierarchy." And this was seen as one nine month old Pakistan baby had attempted murder charges dropped against him and his 12 family members for throwing rocks at the police.   And it is also evident that there are clear differences in the Sharia law verses the laws based on Judea Christian ethics as our United States laws are and as most of England's court systems are also based on the Judea Christian ethics laws.

He was also right in that the world at times can seem smaller as world population grows and the amount of food and water are less and less. A famine would definitely be a cause for a clash of civilizations!   Pastor Rod Parsley stated that "it is better to die by the sword than to die by famine" but in all reality if everyone believed that then they would not persecute Christians because God means what HE says when HE says in Psalm 105:15 "Touch not mine anointed and do my prophets no harm. Moreover the Lord called for a famine and HE brake the whole staff of bread"

I can only hope and pray that Samuel Huntington was wrong but I believe that Abraham Lincoln would have agreed with Huntington's thesis from the famous words of President Lincoln "America will never be destroyed from the outside. If we falter and lose our freedoms, it will be because we destroyed ourselves.

What can we do as Christians? We can live a life according to the Godly principals established in the Holy Bible so that our prayers our not hindered, we can make sure that we are about our Father's business rather than our own, we can also fast and pray more according to HIS word so that we will see more of HIS works in the world today and hopefully more conversions as our lives reflect Christ and we can do our best to be salt and light in our communities. It might not be so hard to do on the East Coast. But in California, New York, Florida and many other places here in America being a Christian in word and deed is truly rare and if there are any … I doubt you will find them! But we must not lose hope. Rather spur one and other on to faith and good works through unity of the brethren.

We can also strive to bring justice to those in the world who have been wronged or exploited by other culture groups, Colonization or Westernization. Strive to be peace makers in the world rather than oppressors, givers rather than takers, friends rather than enemies just as Mother Theresa and Princess Dianna did. Especially in lieu of the economic regionalism that continues to threaten more internal and even global devolution against other economic states and/or regions.
I believe when people (regardless of color, culture, ethnicity, or monetary status) believe that an individual or a group truly has their best interest at heart that they would

never feel the need to defend their selves or offend their selves either.

Some are clever in regards to warning us of our past mistakes with social unrest, civil wars and world wars. I can only pray the right people will recall the tragedies & endless expenses and pay attention. Although I am not sure that the fear of calamity is enough to stop the rages of greed. I am grateful for those who have thoughts of consideration and peace in their views regarding our world today.

Worthy and plausible cause were inscribed in the Latin words "e pluribus unum" which translates to "Out of many, one." of the American coins that our fore fathers endeavored to persuade on a global scale. One worthy of "Ole Glory" and our pledge to the allegiance of the United States of America – the greatest land I know and love. However, as I grew older and learned of all the exploitation of the poor by one global state to another, and as I learned of the differences in world religions that are so important to some who are extremely religious (according to the actions required for some to perform to satisfy their rules) I realize that not everyone may hold those same endearments as closely to their hearts as the fore fathers did.

According to one of our fore fathers President Abraham Lincoln even stated that the possibility to falter would be because we were divided within our own nation state. We have people from every nation in this country but some of those very people may feel indifferent than that motto on the coin I am very sad to say. At the time this great country was birthed that was the farthest from the truth because people were ecstatic to come here! Anyone who came to these shores or borders was considered the happiest and most blessed people in the whole world. If only that were true today than we would be the most glorious people in the world because of our jubilant hearts from a nation at peace. We would not be a Nation that has had to defend herself through war for the past decade.

Considering Cultures & Communities

Language is very important when it comes to evangelism in any culture even if you don't require a translator. You cannot go to a pop culture or rock culture and speak to them the same way that you would speak at a church function. To have the ear of the listener than you must know their lingo or language. And be able to communicate with them in a way that they understand.
To a Christian author that may mean that you have to get your books and writings published in their language if it is a foreign language. To an individual who wants to reach a person who is of a different culture than a love for that other person or that other culture would be important. It would also be best if knowledge of the environment were known and understood by the evangelist.

Some areas that I've traveled on the Southern border of Texas are known to be extremely violent and hostile towards any other culture that is not the drug or Mexican-gang related culture. There is also an active participation in *Santería* where they practice animal sacrifices and other witchcraft ceremonies. To know and understand the environment is important for an evangelist. Anyone who would want to evangelize there should be equipped in spiritual warfare and he must be able to carry his own weight.

Terrain is also another important factor along with lifestyle. For example there are places that are located in the desert regions. And there are cultures that are situated in a party or gambling environment around casinos, alcohol and even brothels like the ones in Nevada. So attire is very important to be able to survive 118 degree temperatures that are daily throughout the summer months in places like Arizona or Palm Springs, California. And to understand the spiritual needs of someone who is addicted to gambling, sex or alcohol may also be important for evangelizing an area bombarded with Casinos and brothels.

Sometimes you can also find communities that have developed into homosexual communities or where nudity is practiced and accepted in their culture. There is a nude culture on the East Coast where a pastor was even preaching nude behind the pulpit. I think it is sad but it happened anyway right here in America. And there are communities that walk across skywalks that were built for gay men to walk across public roads in the nude and that too is happening right here in Southern California. So there are many things that have to be considered when attempting to evangelize a community or culture but I think the very most important asset to have is love. Love for Christ and love for mankind is what is needed most of all.

We are so blessed to have our armed forces on the front lines representing our country. Thank you to all of our military for your hearts of compassion towards those across the world. Love love for humanity truly is the main thing that is needed to bring world peace today. As Christians we should perform the Lausanne Covenant the way that you have done. It does not come naturally to love so freely and with so much innocence. Thank you for your service to God and to our country.

You may count your self blessed to live in such a nice environment that is mainly Christianity! Especially if you take in consideration other parts of the East Coast of the United States and parts of Florida that believes that nudity on the public streets is a way of life for them. And there is even one pastor that preaches in the nude from behind a pulpit. Or take in consideration the casinos, brothels and ungodly sexual relations that are practiced in other communities in Nevada and Southern California. I agree that we should respect the way that others are living and if we want to reach them with the gospel that we should consider their way of living first. When there is a sincere love for any people than there should be nothing to hinder us from attempting to reach them through Christ Jesus. Sometimes just our actions are needed to represent HIM even if it just means being there for someone who is going through a loss of some sort.

Drug Use In Our Society

Reasons for Drug Use in Our Society

When alcohol, drug use or cigarettes are used in the home of a child it kind of gives the wrong signal to the child telling them that this is an acceptable lifestyle. Later, when biological addictions become apparent the damage is already done to both the user and the easily influenced child. When the child grows up it is likely that the child will model after their parents unless there is some form of divine intervention.

If that child grows up and becomes a Christian that child will have tools to resist the lifestyle that was so dominating in the child's youth. That person will then learn and know that you don't have to turn to alcohol or drugs to escape reality but they will know that they can turn to Jesus with any needs or concerns that they face in life. They will know that they can cast their burdens upon the Lord and HE will carry all the burdens for them. They will know that they are not to worry but to pray about everything so the need or tendency to use drugs or alcohol is diminished.

' Our society does play a large role in the use of drugs in America. Many drugs are chemically addicting like alcohol, cigarettes, cocaine, and heroin. Pot is not biologically addicting but it is psychologically addicting. Cigarettes, alcohol and pot would be entirely more sociologically addicting in my opinion but that is not the theory that many in the field of study of behaviors are holding. To me, the more sociably acceptable a drug is (i.e.: cigarettes, pot or alcohol were all acceptable in the community where I grew up in the eighties) the more potentially addicting it would be. Cocaine was not as sociably accepted, neither was heroin.

The temperance model of addictions says that to be around a substance is all that is necessary to become a potential addict. The good that may come out of legalizing an illicit drug that is so widely used and medicinally acceptable like Pot is for potential tax gains that could come from taxing the sale of pot. The bad that would come out of legalizing pot or any other illicit drug is we would have a large society that would be using a drug that would make them less useful to be productive citizens and possibly crime could increase, or risky sexual behaviors could increase.

I agree that the sociological theory is the main reason why people abuse drugs. I also agree that social media in advertisement, tv and movies glamorize drugs and alcohol too much without showing the true ugly side effects of drugs and alcohol. I also think that there is not enough emphasis on spiritual healing of drug abuse. The Lord can bring deliverance. I am not going to say that it is easy or that it is soon coming because I know all too well that it took me over five years to be set free after I had become born again even though I cried out to God for deliverance every single day. It took me fifteen years to finally be delivered from cigarettes even though I begged God for deliverance every single day, went to church faithfully, volunteered in the church on a weekly basis, and gave tithes and offerings to the church on a regular basis. None of that was enough to be delivered from the every so wickedly addicting cigarette.

But God finally gave me a way of escape through the nicotine lozenges and the patch. I stayed on them for over a year and then I went to peppermints. That was in 2007 and I still have to keep a peppermint and or gum in my mouth every waking moment of each day. I will not go into the health complications that were caused by me quitting and subsequently getting addicted to peppermints and gum but it was not without other ramifications. The spiritual side of deliverance needs to be displayed as much as they glorify the sin of drug abuse.

Medicinal reasons are the only reasons that one should take drugs. Anything that the body comes in contact with has to be filtered. Once the body comes in contact with too many toxins the body shuts down, develops cancer and breaks. Some people take drugs to get high, or to escape the pressures of reality. When someone truly has the Lord they do not have to turn to drugs to escape any pressure because they can turn to the Lord and HE delivers HIS people from all their troubles. It is illegal to sell or give away prescription drugs or street drugs. The only people who can administer drugs are licensed physicians or nurses and those in the same medical field of health. They must be licensed health administrators to administer drugs of any kind.
Even with acupuncture or Chiropractic care, massage therapy, any of those type of none invasive types of medicine they still must be licensed to administer any kind of treatment. Drugs are very addicting. Even after I was born again it took me five years to change my lifestyle from one that did what everyone else did to one that honored the Lord. It still took me over fifteen years after I was saved to quit cigarettes even though I cried out and prayed to the Lord on a daily basis for deliverance from all of those bad lifestyles.

Jesus Lovers Have Radical Faith

As a born again Christian who practices the gifts of the Holy Spirit....we are admonished in the scripture to do this only in the presence of fellow Christian believers. Because some prayers require extra faith the bible tells us that sometimes fasting is required to be coupled with the prayer.

The bible also says that we are to "tear down strongholds" and Paula White taught me years ago that she grabs things from the spirit by reaching her hands out and taking them by faith in the physical act of her stretching out her hands and grabbing the air and moving it around as she is directed.
This is an act of faith. If we do not have faith we do not please God.

God was a creator and we are formed and made in HIS image therefore we are creators... creators ... inventors... movers... and shakers that is... if you are born again and empowered with HIS HOLY spirit.

 You can call those things that are not as though they were. You can call things into existence just like God did if you have the faith to believe for it and if you are about the father's business... with man it may be impossible but nothing shall be impossible with God.

Don't call Christian's crazy just because they have radical faith. Christians know that the non-believers have not come into the knowledge of the truth so Christians can tolerate the indifference of non believers a bit easier as long as no one is being persecuted that is!

As a born again Christian who practices the gifts of the Holy Spirit....we are admonished in the scripture to do this only in the presence of fellow Christian believers. Because some prayers require extra faith the bible tells us that sometimes fasting is required to be coupled with the prayer.

The bible also says that we are to "tear down strongholds" and Paula White taught me years ago that she grabs things from the spirit by reaching her hands out and taking them by faith in the physical act of her stretching out her hands and grabbing the air and moving it around as she is directed.
This is an act of faith.

 If we do not have faith we do not please God. God was a creator and we are formed and made in HIS image therefore we are creators... creators ... inventors... movers... and shakers that is... if you are born again and empowered with HIS HOLY spirit.

You can call those things that are not as though they were. You can call things into existence just like God did if you have the faith to believe for it and if you are about the father's business... with man it may be impossible but nothing shall be impossible with God.

Don't call Christian's crazy just because they have radical faith. Christians know that the non believers have not come into the knowledge of the truth so Christians can tolerate the indifference of non believers a bit easier as long as no one is being persecuted that is!
http://www.itbn.org/index/detail/lib/Networks/sublib/TBN/ec/9mbTlnNDpYgxL1RFIpW0zYj1RmlwEgk0

Judaism Was Here Hundreds Of Years Before Islāmic Religion

We should be very wise in the way that we evangelize. Actions speak louder than words and they don't necessarily have to be direct interactions with other people but our lifestyles in and of themselves speaks volumes to even people we've never even met.

One thing that I've just learned because of last week's assignments in class is that Muslims believe Christians and Jews have desecrated the Qur'an and I was thrilled to learn that on the World Religion Time Line that we studied at the first of this subterm taught us that Hinduism was the oldest religion and that Judaism came along before Islāmic Religion.

This means that our Holy Bible has not desecrated their text in the Qur'an and the Hadith but all of our historical Dead Sea scrolls and even the Holy Masoretic manuscripts date back to A.D. 900.

And unless they can prove that their Qur'an and Hadith were written before our oldest Holy texts then that means that Surah 2:75 78-79 can be challenged as their truth that they use to accuse the Jews and Christians of sabotaging the Qur'an.

I once had a friend from Iraq. We worked together at El Palacios Mexican restaurant in Jackson, MS. in the mid-eighties. He was a very nice guy and we wanted so much to accept each other that he told me that Allah was one and the same as the God that I serve.

My heart and spirit knew differently even way back

then. But it never stopped us from being the dearest of friends. Things are a bit different now and I am not sure that I would feel as comfortable in that relationship today.

Critical Thinking (Footnotes Included)

Secular Humanism WorldView

Worldview for Secular Humanism concerning origin would say that natural existence that has always been has brought about their being and existence. That all matter in the universe has always been and that they came into existence as a time and chance occurred. Worldview on the identity from a Secular Humanistic thought is very sad in that they think they have no real value other than that of the value of an animal. They think that animals and humans have the same value and that they just exist and that is how it has always been. Mere existence is their central thought towards all life forms and that is the only identity for Secular Humanism.

Purpose and life meaning for Secular Humanism would be not much more than some temporary substance that they would pass on to the next generation. If they were able to gain any knowledge, wisdom or monetary value in this lifetime that it would simply be donated or taught to the next generation that would remain after they were deceased. They would simply teach other students what they learn and pass down the information gained or they would leave a donation to a particular cause that they felt worthy.

The scariest part of a Secular Humanist world view is the question of morality. They simply have no moral conscious at all. A Secular Humanist has the scariest of all religious worldview moral outlooks. To not think one has any boundaries or limits on the actions of one's life is an extremely dangerous threat to any populace or society.

The final destiny of the life of a Secular Humanist would be nothing more than to just simply die off. There is no afterlife for a Secular Humanist. After death then life is completely over for them. They think that they just rot and decay upon the moment of death and that is it.

Christian Worldview

Origin for A Christian is found in Genesis. God created man from dust. Eve formed from Adam's rib and created from the bone of his rib. We were from and created by God. HE knit us together in our mother's womb. Eve was the mother of all human life. God created Eve from Adam's rib. As opposed to a Secular Humanistic Worldview on Origin who just came about as a matter of time and chance.

Identity for a Christian is one held in awe and esteemed with honor among all creation. As we are God's special creation in that we are uniquely created to have fellowship with God and we are the only creation that HE made in HIS image. HE even esteems us higher than all the heavenly hosts of angels. Our Identity for Christians is in Christ Jesus. It is no longer I that lives but Christ Jesus who lives through me. In contrast with a Humanistic Worldview on Identity who think they are nothing more than just another form of life.

Purpose and Meaning in life for the Christian is much influenced by the word of God. It reflects how one would vote on an election where abortion were an issue or where traditional marriage values were an issue. And our purpose is to become like Christ, to live as HE would have us to live, do what HE would have us to do, become what HE would have us to become. Our purpose and meaning would revolve around Christ Jesus. Christians have significant purpose in life but it is so sad for the Secular Humanist who believe they are of no real significance on earth other than any knowledge or monetary value that they can leave behind after they die.

Our moral values are influenced primarily by the word of God. What God esteems and honors is what a Christian should esteem and honor. What God detests and abhors than we should detest and abhor. The word of God should become the foundation for our thoughts and our conscious. If God calls it sin then we too should acknowledge it as sin. We are to be Holy as HE is holy. We are to love and honor HIS word and keep HIS commandments. Christians are people who one can generally feel safe around because you have a sense that they can be trusted since they are accountable to God for their actions. On the other hand it is very hard to think about leaving a child that you love with a Secular Humanistic person who has no sense of right or wrong and has no conscious either.

Our destiny upon our death for the Christian may seem sad at first but when you realize there will be no more persecution for that soul who dwelt in an earthen vessel, there will be no more sorrow for that man of God or woman of God, for that Christian but only a life spent in Heaven with our Savior and Lord who they have spent their Christian lives adoring. For the Christian who dies it is nothing but sweet relief. The Secular Humanist believe that life is all that there is for them and that upon death there is nothing else.

Genesis 2:7
Hebrews 2:7
Genesis 1:27
1 Corinthians 11:1

Galatians 2:20
1 Peter 1:15-17

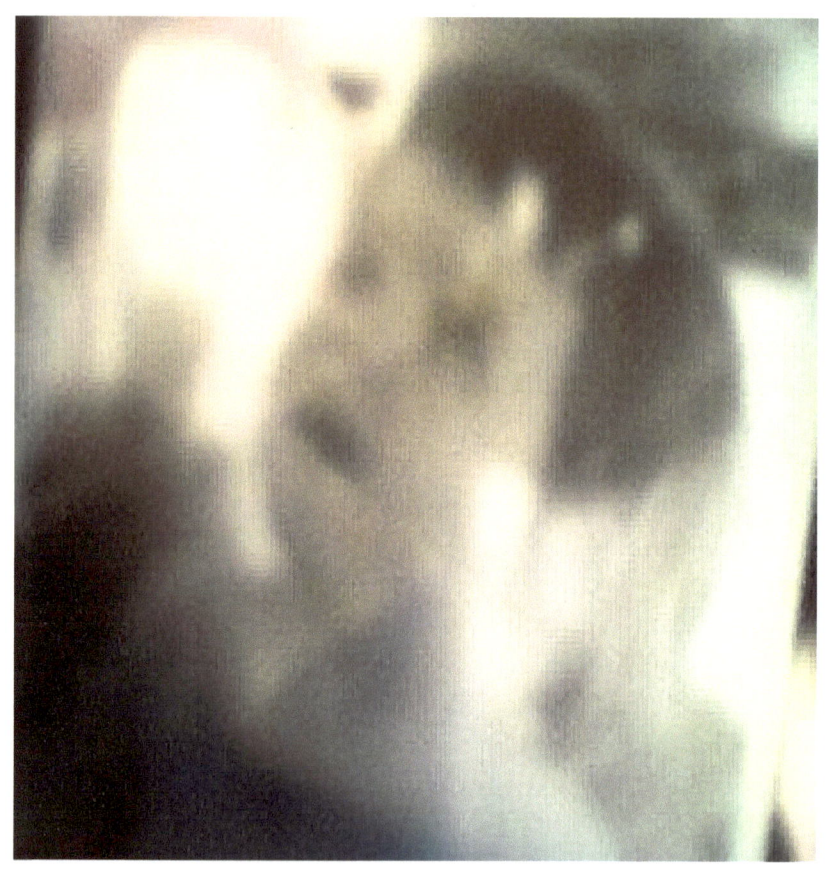

Kimmy Nelson 1 year old

The Problem of Evil

God could have created us to be robots that do exactly what HE wanted us to do but HE would have been so bored. No one would have their own individuality, no conscious to choose from right or wrong and no need for HIS chastisement to show us that HE loves us. John14:15 says "If you love me you, will keep my commandments" and just like with our earthly parents, we are given the choice to obey them or to rebel. Sometimes there are consequences and other times our bad behavior can seemingly go unpunished by our parents.

But as in all areas of life, God has set order to everything. HE chastens those HE loves. "The fear of the Lord is the beginning of all wisdom" Proverbs 9:10 and in Job 28:28 we are told that "the fear of the Lord--that is wisdom and to shun evil is understanding." God gave us a choice. Without evil we would not have the benefit of the choice. Nor would we have the benefit of the blessing because blessing comes by obeying HIS word. See Psalm 119:5 and Ecclesiastes 8:11-12 about how righteousness brings protection and blessing.

We cannot blame all bad things on God. God is only the author of life, good and blessing. If anything bad happens like earthquakes, wars, famines... those are all a result of the fall of Adam. They are a result of sin in this world.

I live in California where we have lots of earthquakes. I also love Science. Take a ball of soft clay then let all the moisture dry out of it like the effects that a drought would have then watch it start to crumble and crack. God promises when HIS people own and possess the land that HE will care for the land and send water in its season. He says this all through Leviticus and Deuteronomy that HIS people have to care for the land like HE tells them to. HE also tells us that HE will send the blessing upon the land of HIS care in Genesis 27:28.

If a drought comes the clay, the earth dries up and shrinks. It becomes condensed in size. Add water or rain and it plumps back up and fills up again. The continued stress on the structure of the ball of clay or the earth will cause an earthquake effect in the earth or a pit or breaking up of the ball of clay. So it is with sin, Sin causes wars because of greed or power. Famines are caused because of greed and lack of responsibility for caring for the earth and God's people. You cannot blame God for man's sin.

The Authentic Living Word Of God

The Word Of God is authentically authored by God for many reasons but the most important one to me is that every time I open the word of God it speaks life to me, it specifically addresses the problem or question that I am seeking the Lord about. This would be argument number four of Dr. Elmer Towns "Ten Arguments for the Word of God"

However that is just one of my personal favorites. I also like Argument number one which is "The Unique Revelation Of Jesus Christ" because this personally may mean something more to me than it does for the next person.

But I know for sure that it was Christ revealing Himself to me as "being alive today" in the day when HE was wooing me unto HIM it was the entire reason that HE was able to reel my heart in. HIS sweet words in the New Testament drew me closer about 6 months after I had experienced the "Born Again" event. But it was HIS undeniable reality of HIS presence in my life that made me fall head over heels in love with HIM.

That is why Dr. Towns is right to ask "If man invented Christ then why didn't man create another?" Or in other words why didn't man "clone" Jesus? That is because just like all of God's creation are unique and irreplaceable. Most especially HIS only begotten SON the only savior of the world, the only one perfect enough to take away the sins of the world, the only one with spotless and sinless blood could redeem mankind for father God.

My second choice for one of Dr. Town's arguments that I will choose is argument number eight: "The Honesty Of The Bible" This is so comforting to me because though

I've lived faithfully and dedicated to the Lord uncompromisingly since 2000 without returning to my former long lifestyle of sin coming from a very paganistic and heathenistic back ground and I didn't come to Jesus until age 28 yet it was five years later before HE purged the world's way of doing things it has not stopped the world from wanting to stone me or throw up my past in my face day in and day out with their Christian persecution.

It is another anchor to my soul knowing that Moses was a murderer, Noah was a drunk, Abraham lied about his wife, Eli didn't discipline his unruly sons, King David (this is my favorite one because he had a heart after God's own heart and I know God was mightily with him) committed adultery.

Though my sins are long gone the world still accuses me, hates me and would love to stone me. And sometimes, their rocks hit me so hard (in the spirit) that I have to convince myself that Jesus loves me and accepts me and that Satan is using them to do his work in attacking me. Then I don't feel so condemned anymore. I like Paul was the chiefest of all sinners at one time... but that was over a decade ago. I have uncompromisingly walked with the Lord through circumstances most would have given up on their faith and said that God didn't keep HIS promises. But like Shadrach, Meshach and Abednigo... my anchor still holds!

Biblical Worldview Essay

Biblical Worldview Essay
By Kimmy Nelson
Theology 104

My degree is in Interdisciplinary Studies with cognates in Health and Social Science. The vocations that I'm already in are internet evangelism, online marketing, publishing and I am an author. The Vocation that God has called me to is in politics.

My business is www.nelsonaffiliates.com and I have three nonprofit organizations that are all housed under "Whole House of the Lord" ministries. First there is my weekly online service ministry www.letshavechurchnow.blogspot.com where I invite the unchurched to attend live services online through my social media posts. The first online ministry that I began is a prolife support ministry http://kimig.tripod.com/america-chose-life.html then later I began a troop support ministry http://militarysupportblog.blogspot.com/

Evangelism
I have been evangelizing on a regular basis for over a decade. My ministry began in the late eighties as I fell in love with Jesus and HIS word. I found myself doing what HE said to do in the word. If someone asks you for the shirt on your back then give them your cloak as well. If someone asks you to go one mile go with them two miles also.
I found myself picking up hitch hikers on my way to church as my home church was down the interstate about five miles. I would tell them that they could get in my car only if they would allow me to take them to church where they could get some cold water and possibly a night at the church shelter. I did this for about three years totaling about

40 hitch hikers. One of them was baptized. He was a really tall Native American Indian man.

Later, my protégé Mother Nell Summers suggested that I do not pick them up anymore as it was just not safe. She suggested that a man should be in that ministry and not a woman. In my books that I author there are many references to God in the book of Poetry. And one of my books is titled "The Successful Single Life" and it tells how to live above reproach as a single Christian. It gives reference to the book of Joshua and many other scriptures that led to my final victorious single life rather than the one I had lived in my late twenties.

God's Purpose for My Life

God has given me divine revelation that HIS will for me is to run in politics. I am a strange bird when it comes to politics because the most important issue to me is prolife. However, I also think that traditional marriage between a man and a woman needs to be preserved. And I know that God has given man dominion over the earth (Genesis 1:28) so it is our responsibility to keep the planet in good health condition. Which is another reason why I support ecofriendly environments that are maneuvered with renewable or clean energy as opposed to oil or petroleum operated vehicles.

I also support sustainability environments so that we can take good care of our planet. As well as complete recycling, reusing, and reducing of materials that are not so easily biodegradable. At some point we should begin to prohibit the use of such materials. I support stronger laws that govern global polices concerning hazardous materials such as chemical, biological, and nuclear waste.

God says that we are to care for the poor and to help the needy (Psalms 82:3) and that we are to be merciful and to execute justice (Micah 6:8). And that we are to refuse bribes and extortion (Isaiah 33:15). We are also to speak up for those who have no voice. We are to love God and our neighbor as our self. Luke 10:25-37 exemplifies the loving of our neighbor. Even when traditionally they are two ethnic groups who are not accustomed to socializing. When we see anyone in need (even if it is your enemy) we are to be kind and gracious unto them. We are to love our enemies and bless those who curse us.

Too often when people are elected into office they see all the corruption that is going on behind closed doors and on every corner and then they compromise and begin doing the same. Some have rejected the ways of average politician and they have held their office with great integrity. That is how the office of a leader should be held is for one to do the right thing even when no one is looking. Not to lie or steal, not to accept bribes or gain from extortion. This cannot be an easy thing to do when so many people are doing it. But when one has been regenerated by the Spirit of God then HE will enable HIS servant to walk honorably among men.

Conclusion

When we have been regenerated by the Spirit of the Lord we are able to live among men honorably in obedience to HIS word so that we will not freely lie, steal, cheat or commit any other sins as others in the world may do. We then have the power to do the right thing when no one is looking. No matter what our vocation if one has been born again then it is likely that same one will want to live a life pleasing unto the Lord. One that would likely conduct their life as Jesus would have done if HE were still on the earth today.

There is an ole cliché that was once popular in the eighties and they made wrist bands out of the slogan "What Would Jesus Do" in the initials "WWJD". I believe that sums up the Christian Worldview Lifestyle.

Why the Church Is Misunderstood

Why the Church Is Misunderstood I believe that this is because there are modern day Ahab's, modern day Jezzabelle's and modern day Eli's who are greedy and could care less about the issues that are profoundly important to the heart of God such as taking care of the widows and orphans. Executing justice, extending mercy, feeding the hungry, clothing the naked…. and so on.

The shepherds have been worthless devouring all the meat offerings and good grain, drinking freely of clean water and then trampling the remaining clean water so that the flock have nothing left to eat or drink. Many shepherds butted with flank and shoulder the weak of the flock. They never searched for the weak or the lost sheep of their pasture. And if they found them they bullied them around hoping that they would go away and not be so troublesome to them. They did not care for the souls of their flock.

They were not good watchmen over the flock. I agree with Dr. Elmer Towns about the church needs to display love towards one and other so that the world can see our love for each other rather than the back biting, fighting and devouring of each other that has been going on for over a decade. I also agree with Dr. Towns that the church needs to repent. Perhaps if the church repented then God could bring revival and pour out HIS spirit upon the church and renew them.

Repentance is the main key otherwise they are wasting their time no matter what good works they do. I also believe that there are individuals in the Bible belt who say that they are Christians but they do not have a problem stealing, lying, cheating, accepting bribes and accepting gains from extortion. Why would I say such a thing? Because this week it was reported that Mississippi is the most corrupt state in the union. Mississippi is in the Bible belt. So obviously there was someone pretending to be a Christian but they were living a dishonorable life before God.

Your Divine Purpose In This Life On Earth

Did you know that you were divinely created by the creator of the universe to solve a problem in this life on this earth in your generation that no one else will ever be able to do but you. Some people go through their whole lives never knowing, never asking, and never being told what their entire life's purpose is.

That almost happened to me. I went to Bartending School in 1986-87 and became a bartender for a brief period of my life. Then I went through 3 years of premed and social science in the early nineties, became a life insurance agent in the late nineties, gave birth to four children between 1980 and 1994. But in 2005 I heard God clearer than I've ever heard HIM before.

He told me that my life's purpose was in politics. I think my dear blessed mother knew this all along somehow as I recall her going and buying me a brand new crimson blouse and set of blazer pants to go with it for my sixth grade class trip from Marshall, MO. to the Missouri State capitol in Columbia. That was one of the few new outfits that I can ever remember getting in my life.

I still think she knew somehow. Maybe it was because I had a paper route early on in my life during that same year. I had an older sister and two baby sisters but out of all four of us I was the only one that ever took up a paper route. That was my first experience with public policy.

I encourage you to seek God for the divine reason and purpose HE has created you for. I can assure you there is one. And it may not and it likely is not in the field that you are currently in. But it is never too late with God for HE will always make a way for you to complete the work that HE created you for.

Let Freedom Ring!

Most people probably take me for an ole stick in the mud type character... a real party pooper. But, the truth is *I am a LIBERTY LOVER*!
In my heart of hearts I believe that all people should have the freedom to live however they want to live just as long as they don't try to push it off on other people.

Freedom to live however one chooses is what has made America great all these years and that should never change.
If people want to smoke dope let them smoke dope till they are blue in the face. If they want to be gay well let them be gay.

Everyone one has to learn from their own mistakes. None of us have ever lived a 100% all of the time spotless and perfect life. And thankfully people change. I'm living proof of that!

However, I do believe that as a government, a church or a community we can set standards and as parents we can teach our children early on what God honors and what HE disdains.

I used to do things that I don't do now and I don't want to be anywhere around anyone who is doing it... YET, I would never assume the responsibility to tell anyone how they should live their lives. Let them live how THEY choose to live.

With only one exception; The Holy Bible. I do believe that we as HIS people have the responsibility to implement HIS commands and HIS laws if they are being challenged. For example; In Mississippi we used to have the "*Blue Light Law*" on Sundays when no alcoholic beverages were allowed to be sold. I think it is an honorable thing that Chick-fil-A is doing by honoring the Sabbath to the best of their knowledge and ability.

Not how you choose for them to live. As long as everyone obeys all the laws and doesn't hurt anyone then you really don't have a single thing to complain about! When it is in your soul "Give me freedom or give me death" you will never assume the responsibility to try and tell others how they should or should not live (if you are not raising children or married to an alcoholic!) Let them live and learn~

What If The Cultural Clash Is Within Your Family?

Domestic Violence Is Bad Apple & A Vicious Cycle That Has To Be Broken

When a man is the head of the household and he abuses a child ... everyone else in that household follows suit because he is the head of the household. Stay away from abusive men.. RUN, RUN, RUN and never look back!

What starts at the top always flows downward? #Leadership If the leader is corrupt then his administration will follow suit. As it goes with the church so will it go with the nation?

 Sometimes, you can tell the character of a man by the look on his wife's face. If she is sad all the time or looks uneasy she may be married to an abusive man.

Abuse is more than physical. If you tell someone that they are only tolerating you because they have to ... That is mental abuse.

If someone calls you a name; dummy, stupid, whore etc.... that is verbal abuse.

If they won't let you use the phone to talk to your mother... that is mental abuse... and can be used against you in a court of law!!!

I've seen it before... men who take advantage of little teenage girls or other women by making them feel that they are the only girl or woman in the world. The most beautiful female on the planet... until they can steal their virginity. They will do anything they can to get in the girl's britches including photo shots, modeling, sketching and paintings of her or even mural of her.

Then when they get her to pose for him, they convince her to start baring more flesh. Then when He strikes his move to steal her virginity he shoots the whole thing on spy cameras only to sell it for porn.

And she falls for it thinking that he truly cares for her. When all along all he wanted was some sex and to make a porn movie that he can sell forever more to the most gullible buyer. Again this is abuse!!!

You know, when people don't care if you die because of hardships of homelessness for over 5 yrs. after stomping all over you for your entire life.

And professional counselors (in my case it was my marriage counselor) tell you that it is because of the root cause of their (with me it was my step father) abuse to you is the reason you chose abusive men.

It might be time to draw the line and let them know where you stand.

My family learned how to abuse me from a very young age by the head of the household when I was a child as far back as when it began at age 2 years old.

But Now, I got another daddy!!! And HIS name Is ABBA Father!

- See more at:
http://faithfreedomforever.blogspot.com/2012/11/domestic-violence-is-bad-apple-vicious.html#sthash.8J7fnhR7.dpuf

More Cultural Clash Is Within The Family

I just unloaded all the pain that was the root cause of me wanting to escape life day and night every waking moment of my teenage years... The Pain (Chains are) is GONE... I've Been Set Free... My God my savior has ransomed me... And like a flood HIS mercy rains unending love amazing Grace!!!"

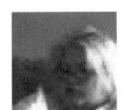

If we don't learn to cast the whole of our burdens, our pain and our cares upon the Lord then we will have to bare them ourselves. That is one load that I don't want to carry. Sometimes family scars can be so deep and so raw that it hurts to even see or talk to a family member at times. Sometimes even when one is dead and gone their wounds can still be as fresh and hurtful as they were the night they inflicted them. This Psalm was written about someone who was at one time real close to the writer of the Psalm, but it is obvious that the author had suffered because of the long time abuse.
Psalm 129
A song of ascents.

1 "They have greatly oppressed me from my youth," let Israel say; 2 "they have greatly oppressed me from

my youth,
but they have not gained the victory over me. 3
Plowmen have plowed my back and made their furrows
long. 4 But the Lord is righteous; he has cut me free
from the cords of the wicked." 5 May all who hate Zion
be turned back in shame. 6 May they be like grass on
the roof, which withers before it can grow; 7 a reaper
cannot fill his hands with it, nor one who gathers fill his
arms. 8 May those who pass by not say to them, "The
blessing of the Lord be on you; we bless you in the
name of the Lord.

- See more at:
http://faithfreedomforever.blogspot.com/2012/11/my-chains-are-gone-ive-been-set-free-my.html#sthash.5TpVbO4g.dpuf

Vote Yes To God

Some may think that they must vote on a certain ticket to protect their best interest. If we do not vote to support God's values on the right to life by protecting the unborn from those who would slaughter the helpless, and by protecting the traditional marriage that God's word honors between one man and one woman then we will lose the liberties to speak out against those things in the future.

Our "Freedom of Speech" along with our Christian lifestyle of church and prayer will lean towards the Nazi Hitler Socialist Communistic country and anti Christ regime that was Ice cold towards God. Worse yet, you may become martyrs for your faith as they have in many other anti Christ nations. God sets the moral ethics, principals and standards for HIS guide lines in the word of God. He clearly tells us that HE "HATES" the shedding of innocent blood

Proverbs 6:16-19

New International Version (NIV)

[16] *"There are six things the LORD hates,*
    seven that are detestable to him:
[17]   *haughty eyes,*
    a lying tongue,
    hands that shed innocent blood,
[18]   *a heart that devises wicked schemes,*
    feet that are quick to rush into evil,

¹⁹ *a false witness who pours out lies*
  and a person who stirs up conflict in the community."

And that He made male and female:

[Genesis 1:26-28](#)

New International Version (NIV)
²⁶ **"Then God said, "Let us make mankind in our image, in our likeness, so that they may rule over the fish in the sea and the birds in the sky, over the livestock and all the wild animals,[a] and over all the creatures that move along the ground."**

²⁷ **So God created mankind in his own image,**
  in the image of God he created them;
  male and female he created them.

²⁸ **God blessed them and said to them, "Be fruitful and increase in number; fill the earth..."**

If you re elect someone who opposes God's standards as often and as strongly as Obama has then the Christian will be the outcast in this nation. And there are Christians in this nation who are already being persecuted for their faith. How much worse will it get if you reelect a president who extremely promotes abortion along with promoting gay marriage?

[I put my money where my mouth is!](#)

- I put my money where my mouth is just like I did when I was in college with three small children at home with me as a single mother when my black Nigerian neighbor who was my friend knew that I was Christian and she asked if her sister could stay with me when she arrived from Nigeria with her two year old son who was coming to America for life saving surgery. I said yes, against my very own mothers will. But the lady who came from

Nigeria was pregnant and she became my very first prayer partner. She was a very dear friend to me otherwise I would have NEVER let her stay in my home while I was gone all day with my children. She stayed with us over three months. Her other son was born in my home.

For the record, (and I have about seven yrs. of these same type bank receipts but my giving of tithes and offerings dates back all the way to 1988) every place you see the word "Breakthrough" on this record of the first seven months of this year history of my giving tithes and offerings to God and alms to the poor that is when every single penny of my money was given only to help those in Sudan, or Haiti. All the information is listed and they can all testify to this truth. And from 2000-2005 I had a youth ministry that consisted mostly of black children who I adored and loved as my very own. Weekly they would come to my house and I would feed them with my food. I took them to the beach with me, to the YMCA, to church, almost everywhere I went they were with me. They stayed the night with me many times and I treasured those children. I am going to gladly share some of the photos with you. But I have lots more if you need them!
https://picasaweb.google.com/117869302152031191697/YouthMinistry?authuser=0&feat=directlink And I still have really dear black friends on Facebook that I love.

Bank records:
10/01/2012 $85.00 10/09/2012 CBL919NH PASTOR SERGIO DE LA MORA
WWW.TURNINGTHEARTS.com
09/27/2012 $12.43 10/04/2012 RBF9O9IG STEVE MUNSEY FAM
09/10/2012 $10.00 09/17/2012 3BI9Y929 Breakthrough
09/06/2012 $10.00 09/13/2012 AB99KA2S LANCE LEARNING G
09/04/2012 $55.00 09/11/2012 CBR92AWU PASTOR

SERGIO DE
09/04/2012 $25.00 09/11/2012 5B69DAWU STEVE
MUNSEY FAM
08/14/2012 $6.00 08/21/2012 LBV9FAW8 BENNY
HINN MINIS
08/13/2012 $5.00 08/20/2012 JBW9UAZI Trinity
Broadcas
08/06/2012 $12.00 08/13/2012 EBC9TADG
Breakthrough
08/06/2012 $4.00 08/13/2012 IBQ9VARG STEVE
MUNSEY FAM
08/01/2012 $86.00 08/08/2012 YBJ9RAXE
SOUTHWEST COMMUNITY CHURCH
(SADDLEBACK Sister)
07/23/2012 $5.00 07/30/2012 RBF9VAO9 Trinity
Broadcas |
07/02/2012 $54.17 07/10/2012 8B5B8S7Y
Breakthrough
07/02/2012 $40.00 07/10/2012 EBUBMSNL STEVE
MUNSEY FAM
06/04/2012 $5.00 06/11/2012 VBPB7SJ1 Trinity
Broadcas
06/04/2012 $3.00 06/11/2012 DBGBVSC1 STEVE
MUNSEY FAM
06/04/2012 $84.00 06/11/2012 OB3BOSTC Roys Desert
Reso
06/04/2012 $4.00 06/11/2012 2BPB7SJ1 Breakthrough
05/29/2012 $5.00 06/05/2012 NBOBSQTT
Breakthrough
05/01/2012 $86.00 05/08/2012 QB6BTQUF STEVE
MUNSEY FAM
05/01/2012 $1.00 05/08/2012 KBHBTQUF Trinity
Broadcas
04/30/2012 $8.22 05/07/2012 GB2B5Q74 STEVE
MUNSEY FAM
04/16/2012 $12.00 04/23/2012 YBJBZQMA STEVE
MUNSEY FAM
04/16/2012 $1.00 04/23/2012 XBJBZQMA Trinity
Broadcas

04/02/2012 $46.00 04/09/2012 JBRBITZM
Breakthrough
04/02/2012 Recurring Payment † $84.00 04/09/2012
HBWB4TSX Free Chapel
03/09/2012 $3.70 03/16/2012 GBKBJTY4 Trinity
Broadcas
03/07/2012 $84.00 03/14/2012 VBQBWTVE Free
Chapel
03/07/2012 $28.00 03/14/2012 LBCBFTJE Trinity
Broadcas
03/05/2012 $84.00 03/12/2012 YBDBLPHM
SOUTHWEST COMMUN
03/01/2012 $1.00 03/08/2012 CBYB4TT1 Breakthrough
02/21/2012 $6.00 02/28/2012 QB5BLPQP Breakthrough
02/10/2012 $18.94 02/17/2012 SBIBQPEX
GUIDEPOSTS / POS
02/06/2012 $20.00 02/13/2012 OB3BVP9K
Breakthrough Paid
02/01/2012 $86.00 02/08/2012 ABXBTPEI
SOUTHWEST COMMUN
02/01/2012 $1.00 02/08/2012 NBMBTPEI Trinity
Broadcas
01/10/2012 $10.00 01/18/2012 UBJBIPY9 Jackson
Revival
01/09/2012 $6.00 01/17/2012 YB8B9P3A Breakthrough
01/03/2012 $12.00 01/10/2012 6BMBUUSO STEVE
MUNSEY FAM
12/30/2011 $1.00 01/09/2012 EBRBLUTV Trinity
Broadcas
12/30/2011 $3.20 01/09/2012 3B1BLUTV Breakthrough
12/30/2011 $3.00 01/09/2012 MB1BLUTV STEVE
MUNSEY FAM
12/29/2011 $3.20 01/06/2012 KBSBMU4V
Breakthrough 12/13/2011 $10.00
12/06/2011 $12.42 12/13/2011 WBSBWUYG
Breakthrough
12/05/2011 $3.00 12/12/2011 WBOBSU95 STEVE
MUNSEY FAM
12/01/2011 $1.00 12/08/2011 3BZBXUKE Trinity

Broadcas
11/29/2011 $1.50 12/06/2011 FBXB8UYD
Breakthrough Paid
11/29/2011 $1.50 12/06/2011 7BXB8UYD STEVE
MUNSEY FAM
11/08/2011 $7.00 11/16/2011 JB3BUOKV Trinity
Broadcas
10/25/2011 $1.00 11/01/2011 WBFB4O78 Trinity
Broadcas
10/25/2011 $7.00 11/01/2011 MBFB4O78 Breakthrough
10/20/2011 $5.00 10/27/2011 VB8BLOIH Free Chapel

Youth Ministry

picasaweb.google.com

Photos by Kim Gerred, Jun 26, 2008 - Tarpon Springs,
Florida 2000-2005

Over 80% Of the Children in my care (some
photographed above) were Colored Or Hispanic. I
considered them my children because I loved them as
my own. Approximately 75 Children In Florida between
2000-2005 And About 25 More Children in TX., MS., &
MO. between 2006-2010

 I have felt prejudice coming from the black culture
against the white man. As I waited over 3 yrs as the only
homeless white woman of four children including one
baby in 1994-1996 with no help from HUD or any other
housing agency. And I have felt prejudice from the
Spanish culture toward the white man as the only white
disabled homeless woman in a shelter on the border of

Mexico in Laredo, Texas (99% Spanish Community and over 65% could not speak English) in 2006 when the shelter gave semi permanent housing to illegal immigrants but would not give it to me. It did not matter that it was in the U.S.A. or that I was the only natural and legally born American there or that I was disabled and had been very sick, it didn't even matter that I had already spend two years homeless prior to my coming to that shelter. . They did not help me. Was it because I was not Mexican? Only God knows!

Not all Mexicans are prejudice and not all black people are either. I have great friends in the black race here in America who I love and treasure their friendships. Some of which have had their children over to stay the night at my house when their children were only babies. I also have dear friends from South Of the border who are my best friends. I have spent the night with them many times and gone to Mexico with them for day break vacations. Or gone to dinner with them over in Mexico where her husband was the manager of a nice authentic Mexican restaurant where I was served real cantaloupe juice with my dinner and I loved it! I considered her my best friend. I would have never spent the night with her many times or ever gone to Mexico with her had I even suspected she had bad intentions towards me.

But there have been some in leadership where I used to live in MS that bullied me around in the system because I was a poor white woman in a city of 95% blacks. Now the stats have gone up for Jackson, MS. and it is more like 99% black population. Let me just say this... I don't care what color you are or where you are from ... if you hate another race be it white, Mexican or black ... I can tell you right now that you are not right with God. God is the avenger and HE will repay!

1st Sunday School Lesson I Taught In Laredo, TX 2006 (ages 9-18) Vam & Zohn's Church

If you have young children ages 12-18 here are the verses that you can easily teach them to help them make the best choices in their future lives. They will also help protect them from the evils of this world and from diseases caused by sexual immorality.

James 1:6 "But if any of you lacks wisdom, let him ask of God, who gives to all generously and without reproach, and it will be given to him

. King James Bible"

Job 28:28 And unto man he said, Behold, the fear of the Lord, that is wisdom; and to depart from evil is understanding.

Joshua 1:7-8 "Be strong and very courageous. Be careful to obey all the law my servant Moses gave you; do not turn from it to the right or to the left, that you may be successful wherever you go. 8 Keep this Book of the Law always on your lips; meditate on it day and night, so that you may be careful to do everything written in it. Then you will be prosperous and successful."

Many kids have been influenced or introduced into gang communities. Most of the children who are in those gangs or who were ever attracted to that lifestyle were also struggling in the area of finances. Some may have been raised to think that it is okay to steal to get what they want. That is not the truth. When they steal or lie that could open the door to bring the curse upon them. It is when they live according to the principals of the bible and the Ten Commandments that the blessing comes but that is only if they make Christ Jesus their Lord. He must first be Lord of their lives. There are shorter versions of the Ten Commandments that you can teach your children from but for this teaching we will stick to the version from Exodus 20.

Exodus 20: 1-17 "The Ten Commandments

20 And God spoke all these words:

2 "I am the Lord your God, who brought you out of Egypt, out of the land of slavery.

3 "You shall have no other gods before[a] me.

4 "You shall not make for yourself an image in the form of anything in heaven above or on the earth beneath or in the waters below. 5 You shall not bow down to them or worship them; for I, the Lord your God, am a jealous God, punishing the children for the sin of the parents to the third and fourth generation of those who hate me, 6 but showing love to a thousand generations of those who love me and keep my commandments.

7 "You shall not misuse the name of the Lord your God, for the Lord will not hold anyone guiltless who misuses his name.

8 "Remember the Sabbath day by keeping it holy. 9 Six

days you shall labor and do all your work, 10 but the seventh day is a sabbath to the Lord your God. On it you shall not do any work, neither you, nor your son or daughter, nor your male or female servant, nor your animals, nor any foreigner residing in your towns. 11 For in six days the Lord made the heavens and the earth, the sea, and all that is in them, but he rested on the seventh day. Therefore the Lord blessed the Sabbath day and made it holy.

12 "Honor your father and your mother, so that you may live long in the land the Lord your God is giving you.

13 "You shall not murder.

14 "You shall not commit adultery.

15 "You shall not steal.

16 "You shall not give false testimony against your neighbor.

17 "You shall not covet your neighbor's house. You shall not covet your neighbor's wife, or his male or female servant, his ox or donkey, or anything that belongs to your neighbor."

Proverbs 3: 3-4 "My son, do not forget my teaching, but keep my commands in your heart, 2 for they will prolong your life many years and bring you peace and prosperity. 3 Let love and faithfulness never leave you; bind them around your neck,

write them on the tablet of your heart.
4 Then you will win favor and a good name
in the sight of God and man."

Proverbs 3:7-8 "Do not be wise in your own eyes;
fear the Lord and shun evil.
8 This will bring health to your body
and nourishment to your bones."

Proverbs 3:13-16
13 "Blessed are those who find wisdom,
those who gain understanding,
14 for she is more profitable than silver
and yields better returns than gold.
15 She is more precious than rubies;
nothing you desire can compare with her.
16 Long life is in her right hand;
in her left hand are riches and honor."

Last but not least, Proverbs 8:10-21
10 "Receive my instruction, and not silver; and knowledge
rather than choice gold.

11 For wisdom is better than rubies; and all the things that
may be desired are not to be compared to it.

12 I wisdom dwell with prudence, and find out knowledge
of witty inventions.

13 The fear of the Lord is to hate evil: pride, and arrogancy,
and the evil way, and the froward mouth, do I hate.

14 Counsel is mine, and sound wisdom: I am

understanding; I have strength.

15 By me kings reign, and princes decree justice.

16 By me princes rule, and nobles, even all the judges of the earth.

17 I love them that love me; and those that seek me early shall find me.

18 Riches and honour are with me; yea, durable riches and righteousness.

19 My fruit is better than gold, yea, than fine gold; and my revenue than choice silver.

20 I lead in the way of righteousness, in the midst of the paths of judgment:

21 That I may cause those that love me to inherit substance; and I will fill their treasures."

Names Changed in "Title" for privacy.

- See more at:
http://faithfreedomforever.blogspot.com/2012/10/1st-sunday-school-lesson-i-taught-in.html#sthash.l2xHm6iT.dpuf

Geographical Agriculture Diffusion

I am a vegetarian more than 75% of the time with the exception of Passover, Thanksgiving, Christmas and a few blue moons a year when I take out fast food so I would say that most of the products that I consume have been effected by the geographical agriculture theme of movement. My favorite food is the avocado which has its agriculture hearth in the East and highlands of Mexico. I also love the potato and recently the potato was discovered to provide a lot of antioxidants that are beneficial in fighting carcinogenic like the fertilizers and pesticides called "Roundup" produced by a company mentioned in the book named Monsanto. On that note I will share a bit of home economics with you; when you buy any fruits, vegetables and even beans or lentils it is important that you wash the food well with salt and water.

It is strange how some related the tubular potato to a disease and others thought that tomatoes were poisonous before one brave soul ventured off into the edible fruit and not a vegetable. It is the only one from its nightshade family that is not poisonous. Avocado's and tomatoes are very easy to grow right here in California where I live. Avocados also grow very easily in Florida but the taste is distinctly different and I really don't care for the Florida avocado at all. Tomatoes can even grow from an upside down planter where the dirt is on top and the tomato plant comes out of the bottom of the planter and grows upward producing first little yellow fragile flowers with a wonderful aroma of fresh tomatoes.

The bible actually speaks of rams that come from Bashan in Deuteronomy 32:15 "Butter of the herd, and milk of the flock, with the fat of lambs, (I recently enjoyed the delicious Passover Roasted Shank as I do each year) rams from Bashan, and goats, with the choicest grains of wheat, and of the blood of the grape thou drankest wine" It also mentions eating honey and oil from the crag. I am thankful for the tea that was brought over from East India during the Boston Tea Party when American's dressed as Indians were outraged because of the British "Tea Act" May 10, 1773. I drink tea every day. I love black tea, green tea, rooibos tea, and chai. I also drink herbal teas such as Senna, ginger, licorice and I know many of these herbs are not native to the American soil. I am thankful for having such a great variety that the colonizers first embarked on creating a path for us to have access for other cultural fruits, vegetables, roots, teas, and meats.

CULTURAL CLASH EFFECTS ON THE ENVIRONMENT

Naming Only A Fraction Of The Implications On Earth From Extracting Energy Resources

Now that Putin and China have a pipeline deal that will transport energy from Russia to China Putin can take advantage of this to leverage power in the world. Wars have been fought throughout time over resources. Nations have been plumaged and ravished over energy.

Independence from other nations resources would be idea but if that is not possible than this sort of leverage gets asserted. But not without global risks of pollution or other consequences from tampering with the natural structure of the earth's surface and resources that are deep beneath.

In May, 2014 there was another oil spill but this time it was only 50,000 gallons and they all landed on the streets of Los Angeles. This time it wasn't because of an offshore accident or a train wreck, or even a diesel spill. The oil pipes beneath earth's surface burst causing oil to spew into the atmosphere above the city of Los Angeles then fall back to the ground and run like a river in the streets below.

It was also in May 2014 that the Scientists released documentation linking the groundwater pumping to the increased earth quake activity near the San Andreas Fault line.

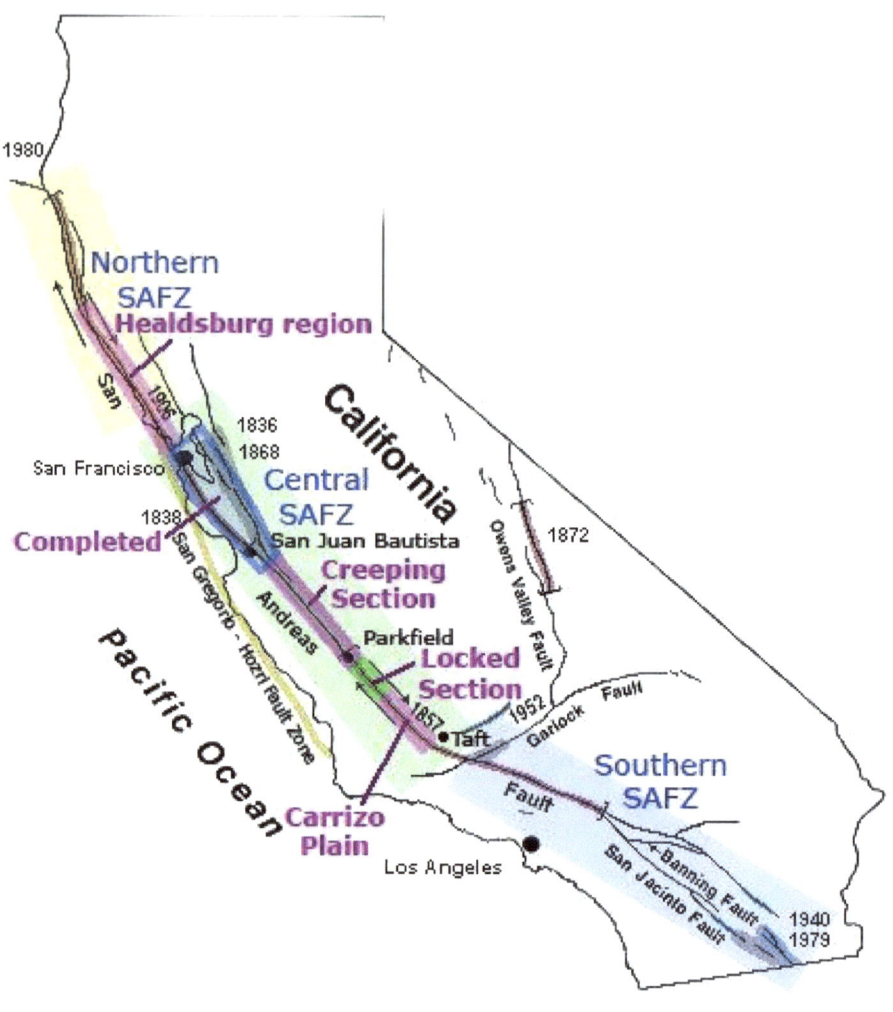

Study reports say "These results suggest that human activity may give rise to a gradual increase in the rate of earthquake occurrence," It was published in the Journal Nature May 2014 written by scientists from Western Washington University, University of Ottawa, University of Nevada, Reno and UC Berkeley.

There needs to be a global monitoring system that polices the pollutants and dangers put forth by the chemicals of any sort and the implications that they have on the earth. There also needs to be global taxing or tariffs on companies and countries who cause damage to earth's surface or below her ocean's floor surface because the damages are virtually irreparable and will cost us all when there is no more oxygen, food or clean water.

Reference

http://www.businessinsider.com/oil-pipe-bursts-in-atwater-village-california-2014-5

http://www.latimes.com/local/lanow/la-me-ln-groundwater-more-earthquakes-20140514-story.html

MINDFUL WASTE

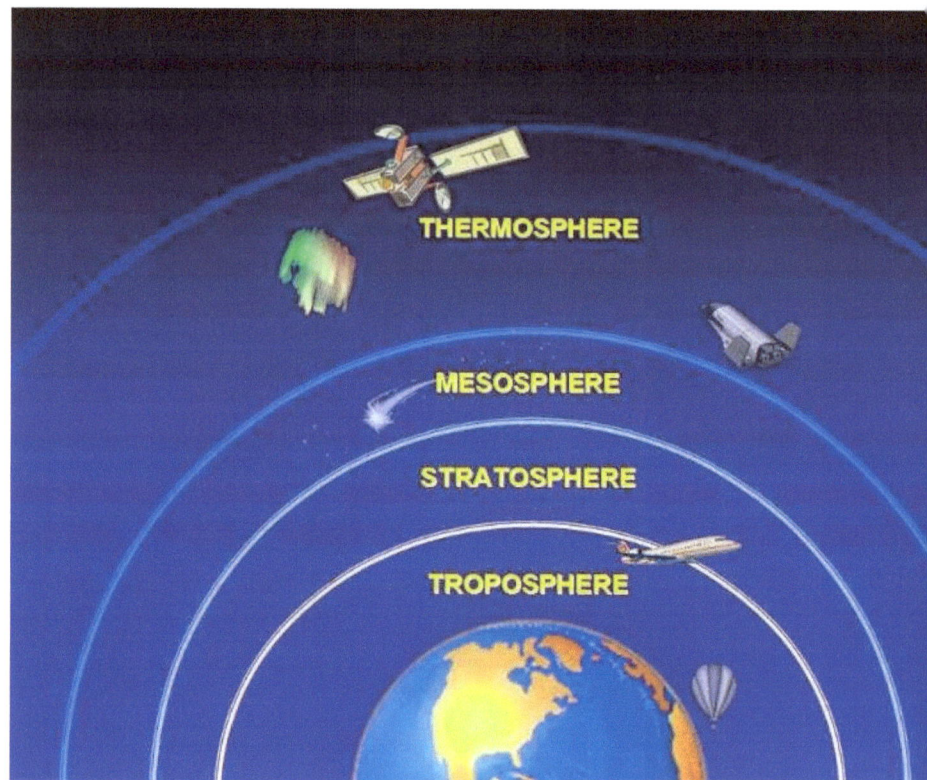

In the last 200 years population growth has increased by four times going from 1 and 1/2 billion to 6 billion in the 20th century alone. Now it is 7 billion since we are in the 21st century. Because of the mass population growth that translates into the greater environmental changes that are likely to occur.

This is all the more reason we need new international limits on toxins and new international legislation on proper waste management, and new regulations on how things are to be disposed of and what can or cannot be disposed.

Poor countries should not be allowed to sale landfills to other countries unless there are stipulations included that prohibit open and unsanitary garbage dumps.
We must drastically reduce the amount of waste that is being produced.

Perhaps there could be another action similar to the Vienna Convention where the Montreal Protocol international agreement was signed in 1987 by 105 countries and the European Community which stopped the ozone layers fast depletion by aerosol sprays and refrigerants.

It is TIME for America and China to sign the Kyoto Agreement Protocol and strengthen the Copenhagen Accord Agreement

http://en.wikipedia.org/wiki/Kyoto_Protocol

http://en.wikipedia.org/wiki/Copenhagen_Accord

http://globalriskinsights.com/

https://maplecroft.com/themes/gr/

http://www.weforum.org/issues/global-risks

http://www.un.org/geninfo/bp/enviro.html

http://www.unep.org/Documents.multilingual/Default.asp?DocumentID=55&ArticleID=274&l=en

http://www.thegef.org/gef/

#green #sustainable #ecofriendly

Wonder why all the starfish are dying by the millions? They now say is is because of a virus. Could it be possible that the virus was initiated by all the pollution?

http://www.dailymail.co.uk/news/article-2550621/MILLIONS-starfish-mysteriously-dying-North-Americas-west-coast.html

One way to get closer to being 100% renewable, recyclable, or reusable is the way that I do it: I've been doing this proficiently for many years now. The only thing that I dispose of that cannot be recycled are things like dirty Q-tips, napkins, paper towels, toilet paper, tea bags, or items that cannot be washed and have food particles on it.

My cans, jars and bottles get cycled through the dishwasher before I recycle them making it easier for the recycle process and that way I can store the recycling in my house without any odor. Everything else gets recycled, reused or renewed in one way or another. I use my tiny applesauce containers as mini ice trays.

One applesauce container is perfect for one glass of water. You only need that one ice cube. Other items that have lids to them are perfect to keep for food storage or even dried herbs or powdered herbs.
http://education.nationalgeographic.com/education/encyclopedia/great-pacific-garbage-patch/?ar_a=1

China Clean Air, Japan & India Energy Independent

By Kimmy D. Nelson

Clean Air & Energy Independent Asia

It should be the goal of every state and every nation to become sustainable, energy independent and free from the control of any other state or nations. And it should be the goal of every nation to be free from any energy dependence to another state or nation's energy leverage. Also for every state and nation to be sustainable with clean air and clean water as a benefit of their success.

By extracting the natural gas resources from China, Japan and India for the use of natural gas operated vehicles, permanent magnetic generators and motors or electromagnetic grid operated trains for all of the major land transportation needs they will begin to have cleaner air and be more independent and sustainable at the same time. All the while the whole world will benefit because of their efforts to reduce greenhouse emissions and improve their global position as a leader in the new world of sustainability for the future survival of life on planet earth.

As they are improving their sovereign global position by becoming energy independent they will improve their financial security as well by reducing the need and cost of imported energy.

Keywords: China, Japan, India, green, greenhouse emissions, emissions, CO2, coral reef, sustainability, imported oil, air quality, ecofriendly, planet, earth

Why Clean Air For China & Why Energy Independence For Japan & India

It is important to try and help China become sustainable and ecofriendly so that they will have cleaner air and less pollution. It is also important to help India and Japan become energy independent all the while making the world a cleaner more ecofriendly environment.

India and Japan are dependent on imported crude oil. India has some natural gas resource in the Western Offshore region. Japan has very little natural gas. China is very dependent on coal and other unclean energy. We are only helping ourselves when we help others to become sustainable and ecofriendly. This will also help end the wearing of face masks or gas masks for millions of people in the nation of China and it will help India and Japan to be free from energy dependence on imported oils.

China Free From Pollution

We will expose how the thick haze over Bo Hai Bay and Yellow Sea is likely due to the industrial pollution in China. And how smog from mainland China has reached California. And how sulfur dioxide emissions have been on the decline since 2006. And how (CFC's) chlorofluorocarbons are responsible for tearing the hole in our atmosphere's protective ozone layer.

And how Anthropocene proves that mankind is responsible for saving or destroying our planet's eco system, our clean air and our clean water. And we must do our part to demand international action be taken to limit or stop all industrial and agricultural pollutants from further destroying our planet.

We can see how enormous quantities of industrial and agricultural pollutants are contributing to the greenhouse effect with their greenhouse gases, carbon dioxide (CO_2), methane, and nitrous oxides and the environmental stresses that they cause. And how they are also contributing to the cause of the hole in the ozone's protective layer in earth's atmosphere. We must now insist that complete recycling, reusing, and reducing must be a global effort while we reduce or completely stop any possible new industrial pollutants from being produced.

Location

The first location is in India we will be discussing for possible conversion all vehicles to use or convert to natural gas, electromagnetic railroads or permanent magnetic generators and motors for vehicles other than manual transportation. There are already some natural gas pipe lines next to Bombay (Mumbai) Latitude 18° 55' N, and Longitude 72° 54' E border that ends or begins there on the Eastern side that runs up through the North Eastern part of India between Pakistan and Nepal that ends and begins in Delhi.

And the location on the main island of Japan for the beginning railroad is at Aomar Japan with a global position of 40.8167° N, 140.7500° E Beijing China's location is 39.9139° N, 116.3917° E.

We will be looking at Beijing because it is one of the top 20 most polluted cities in China.

That natural gas pipe line in Bombay India need to be enlarged to stretch the entire length and width of India's borders and possibly through out several key points inside along the railroads paths. The rail road runs all the way through every direction of India. Perhaps we can look at all the possibilities of extending the uses of the railroad system to include passenger trains and cargo trains and maybe increase the train schedules to make more runs for both passengers and for cargo. This would help reduce the nation's dependency on crude oil.

Japan's main island and her little outskirt islands as well need to start building fusion type reactors. And maybe they can focus on converting all vehicles to permanent magnetic generators and motors. This will end their need for imported crude oil for the nation of Japan and the nation of India since those two nation states are totally dependent on imported crude oil. This will also help tremendously in reducing greenhouse gases, methane, carbon dioxide (CO_2) and nitrous oxides that are polluting the planet's atmosphere.

China must also changes to contribute to reversing the damages caused by their tremendous outpouring of toxins in the planet's environment. Japan and China can begin using steam engines to produce energy and heat without the toxic side effects.

They can help do this by converting some of their industrial plants to be energized by steam engines which are very efficient and a direct energy conversion. This will stop the outflow of the massive poisonous environmental hazards and still provide a way for them to continue their industrial contributions to the world.

And they can also convert some into biofuel research industries and other locations they can convert into fusion type reactor plants. If they build 30 strategically placed fusion type power plants in Tibet, Beijing, Shanghai and all across China that will be sufficient to supply energy for the entire nation of China.

One fusion power reactor could supply all the energy needs for Japan. They must also utilize all their natural gas lines and railroad stations to be the main source of transportation for their country.

.

Place

The place is the continent of Asia for China and Japan and the subcontinent of South Asia for India. China's natural gas is piped in through Miramar Burmese from the Bay of Bengal. Japan has some natural gas but limited. India has a supply of natural gas resource available to them through the Western Offshore regions by Mumbai high complex.

And all three countries have some railroad system already in place. India's rail system is extensive and well-connected throughout the nation. Japan's runs along the coast line in most of the country. China has an extensive railroad system too. Perhaps they can make sure they are using their railroads to do as much passenger and freight uses as
possible.

Movement

These are areas that are already supplied with railroads and with some natural gas pipe lines. However the natural gas pipe lines will need to be enlarged and increased in India. .

Dr. Hans Petermann says "Fusion energy is hydrogen, nitrogen, H20 and oxygen processed at very high temperatures then maintained by stabilizing the temperature to produce a constant supply of energy 24/7 without the toxic waste that nuclear energy, coal and oil produce.

This is done in a fusion reactor that would have to be built and Dr. Hans Peterman can build it. The Germans have already got rid of most of their nuclear energy plants and they have switched to solar energy and natural gas. The fusion process has been known to scientist for many years.

A fusion reactor has to be constructed and built and Dr. Hans Petermann can build it. The fusion reactor which has been accomplished previously in Germany is great to phase out all nuclear power plants and switch over to fusion energy" Dr Hans continues by saying that this fusion reactor fusion energy supplies constant energy can be maintained by regulating the temperature. He said Japan can also do cold fusion like they've been doing by a scientist in France.

Dr. Stanley Pons in 1989-90 and Fleischmann (Fleischmann is now retired) but Pons has continued in the work in cold fusion (a chemical energy process) by using elements by low heat and changing chemicals molecular structure to get energy out.
And Dr. Hans says that Japan and India can also use permanent magnetic generators and motors can be used to run any vehicle. And Japan can use the steam engine for heat and China can use the steam engine for heat. And they can continue to use the electro magnetic
train.

Region

Much of the Continent of Asia is already equipped with natural gas pipelines and railroads. And in the subcontinent of Asia in India they are well equipped with railroads and their own natural gas supply. Japan and China have had lots of interactions between their two countries for centuries. India has also had some influence on some of the areas in and near China.

Human Environment Interaction

Dr. Hans Petermann says that Japan needs to go all solar and natural gas energy for now until a fusion energy reactors can be built which are very safe, reliable and there are no toxic wastes like the billions of tons of nuclear waste that are already being disposed of throughout the world. They are storing the nuclear waste at Yucca Flats Nevada U.S.A. With the Fusion Energy process that will exclude the toxins altogether.

The nuclear waste can be made inert by using brown's gas to neutralize the nuclear waste totally. Dr. Hans Petermann knew Dr. Yull Brown he was originally from Bulgaria.

China must now reverse their damages that they have caused into the earth's atmosphere. They can begin doing research to find out how best to do so but they must also drastically reduce and further limit their industrial and agricultural pollutants. If they want to continue to operate any of their industrial plants they must now convert to the steam engine to produce energy because this will not produce any toxins to the environment. They must now convert to the steam engine.

A highly nuclear radioactive fuel rod from nuclear reactors will remain radioactive for thousands of years if not millennia and must be stored in remote places where they will not contaminate water, air, or any other parts of the eco system's environment.

In all of man's genius inventions we still have not found out how to enjoy this life and be productive by being 100% renewable, recyclable, or reusable. And until life becomes uninhabitable on planet earth or mankind wises up to the fact that is the only way to survive on this planet is by not producing things that you cannot live with or get rid of for thousands of years.

The truth is... nuclear energy should have never been produced. Neither should plastic have ever been produced. But we did now we need to fix it. Either find the antidote or stop producing it whatever the disease, or in this case toxin may be.

In the last 200 years population growth has increased by fourfold going from 1.5 billion to 6 billion in the 20th century alone. Now it is 7 billion since we are in the 21st century. Because of the mass population growth that translates into the greater environmental changes that are likely to occur.

This is all the more reason we need new international limits on toxins and new international legislation on proper waste management, and new regulations on how things are to be disposed of and what can or cannot be disposed.

Poor countries should not be allowed to sale landfills to other countries unless there are stipulations included that prohibit open and unsanitary garbage dumps.

We must drastically reduce the amount of waste that is being produced.
References:

http://upload.wikimedia.org/wikipedia/commons/a/ac/India_mineral_map.jpg
http://maps.unomaha.edu/Peterson/geog1000/MapLinks/Japan.htm

http://en.wikipedia.org/wiki/Pollution_in_China

http://beforeitsnews.com/war-and-conflict/2012/06/a-burmese-solution-to-beijings- south-china-sea-behavior-2279146.html

http://en.wikipedia.org/wiki/Natural_resources_of_India

http://www.eia.gov/countries/country-data.cfm?fips=ja

http://www.businessinsider.com/russia-china-pipeline-2014-5

Dr. Hans Petermann
760-327-4761
P.O. BOX 74
Palm Springs, CA. 92263

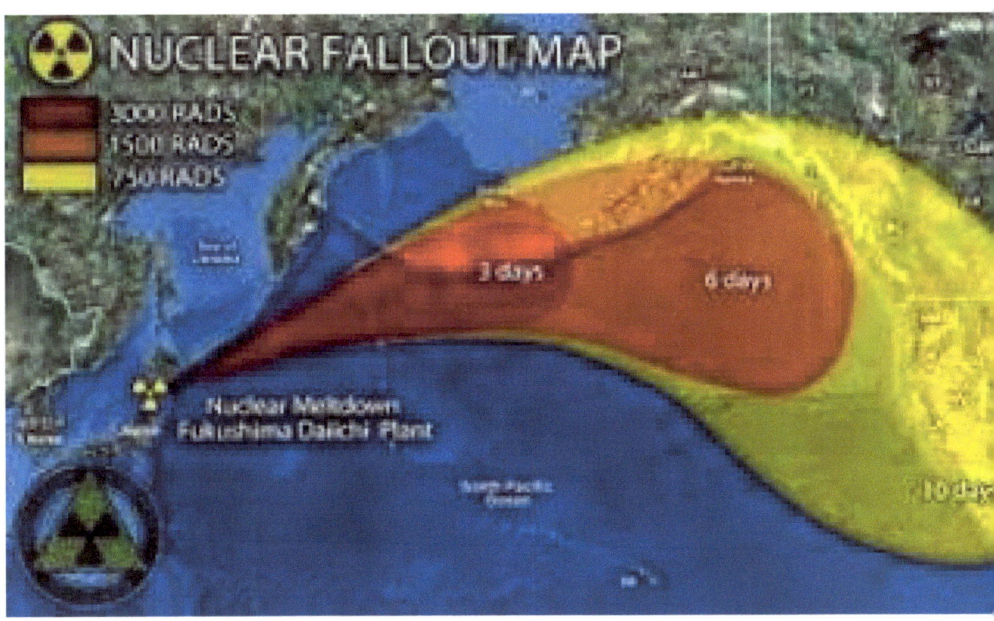

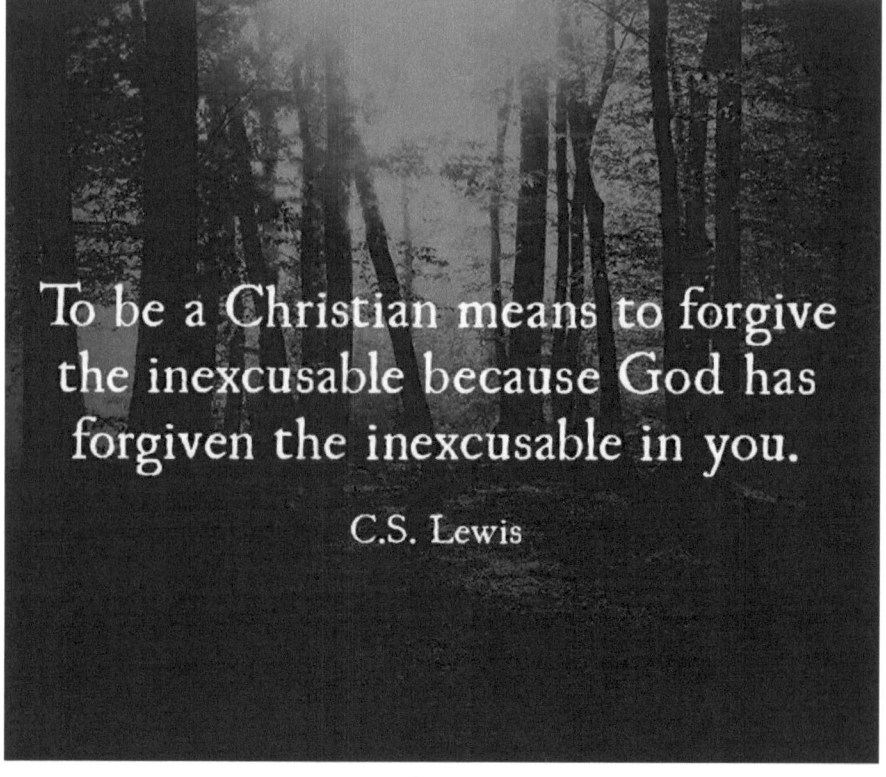

To be a Christian means to forgive the inexcusable because God has forgiven the inexcusable in you.

C.S. Lewis

If we were to walk a mile in everyone's shoes we would see, know and understand why they made every decision and choice they made. I used to have to self medicate and try and escape the reality of what I could not accept or deal with in my home life. I did it for so long that I became addicted to those self destructive behaviors and lifestyles of partying until one day I got saved in 1988. At which point I was so addicted to the only lifestyle I had ever known of partying and self destruction that it took five years for me to finally be delivered from some of the worst parts of it. But it wasn't until 2007 that I was finally delivered from cigarettes. We never know what a person is going through so we should not cast stones. #KeepItReal #Transparent #GlassHouses #Recovery #Addiction #Drugs #Alcohol #DomesticViolence #SelfDestruction

Grab a plate and throw
it on the ground.
- *Ok done.*

Did it break?
- *Yes.*

Now say sorry to it.
- *Sorry.*

Did it go back
to the way
it was before?
- *No.*

Now, do you
understand?

This is much like the one that my mother gave me. Mine had removable hair, the head attached to a cloth body, porcelain head, arms, hands, legs and feet. She had blues eyes with brunette hair. She wore a very fancy blue velvet ball room dance gown. I don't have her anymore for reasons unspoken. #DomesticViolence

LOVE, PEACE And RESPECT

There are many ways that Cultural Clash is relevant to all human life and the planet we live on. The goal should be that we live together keeping our neighbors and this planets best interest in mind when we live and move and have our being on the earth. One way to do that is by implementing the word of God in every aspect of your daily lives. Then you have done your part in making this world a better place to live.

www.ingramcontent.com/pod-product-compliance
Lightning Source LLC
Chambersburg PA
CBHW040310010626
45792CB00022B/31